UNOFFICIAL
GUIDES

21st Century Skills INNOVATION LIBRARY

FORTNITE:
Guide to Chapter 2

800
50
100

CHERRY LAKE PUBLISHING • ANN ARBOR, MICHIGAN

CHERRY LAKE PRESS

Published in the United States of America by Cherry Lake Publishing
Ann Arbor, Michigan
www.cherrylakepublishing.com

Reading Adviser: Marla Conn MS, Ed., Literacy specialist, Read-Ability, Inc.

Library of Congress Cataloging-in-Publication Data
Names: Gregory, Josh, author.
Title: Fortnite. Guide to chapter 2 / by Josh Gregory.
Other titles: Guide to chapter 2
Description: Ann Arbor, Michigan : Cherry Lake Publishing, [2020] | Series:
  Unofficial guides | Includes index. | Audience: Grades 4-6 | Summary:
  "Learn more about Fortnite Chapter 2! Dive in and explore the 13 new
  locations and learn the ins and outs of exciting new challenges. With
  hundreds of millions of players around the world, Fortnite is the video
  game sensation that has taken the world by storm. Its unique design
  combines the construction and problem solving of games like Minecraft
  with competitive online battles. Includes table of contents, author
  biography, sidebars, glossary, index, and informative backmatter"–
  Provided by publisher.
Identifiers: LCCN 2019050074 | ISBN 9781534167247 (hardcover) | ISBN
  9781534167254 (paperback) | ISBN 9781534167261 (pdf) | ISBN
  9781534167278 (ebook)
Subjects: LCSH: Fortnite Battle Royale (Game)–Juvenile literature.
Classification: LCC GV1469.35.F67 G74452 2020 | DDC 794.8–dc23
LC record available at https://lccn.loc.gov/2019050074

Cherry Lake Publishing would like to acknowledge the work of the Partnership
for 21st Century Learning, a Network of Battelle for Kids. Please visit
http://www.battelleforkids.org/networks/p21 for more information.

Printed in the United States of America
Corporate Graphics

Contents

Chapter 1

The End of the World

Fortnite is almost always thrilling to play. It is easy to spend hours on end battling with friends, trying on new **skins**, and exploring the island. But October 2019 was an especially exciting time to be a *Fortnite* fan. That month, one of the biggest events

Chapter 2 gave *Fortnite* a fresh new start that drew in many new players.

Cast/Pull

50
100

XP SUPERCHARGED!

Q

Savage
Danny B

Fishing was one of the many new features added in Chapter 2.

in the game's history took players by surprise. Over the course of just a few days, the world of *Fortnite* was changed forever with the massive Chapter 2 update.

Fortnite changes all the time. New weapons get added, and others get removed. New buildings and environments show up on the island. Sometimes special game modes shake up the way *Fortnite* is played for a few weeks. So what makes the Chapter 2 update so special? Quite simply, it's the biggest update the game has ever seen, and it introduced a lot of changes all at once. Players got a brand-new island to explore, and even the game's Battle Pass system was changed.

It all started as the tenth season of *Fortnite*'s first chapter was drawing to a close. Over the course of the season, familiar old buildings and other landmarks had started popping up all over the *Fortnite* island. These structures had been added and removed from the island during previous seasonal updates. But now they were appearing again. It seemed like they were showing up thanks to mysterious portals called rifts.

Rifts formed in the sky above the island near the end of Chapter 1.

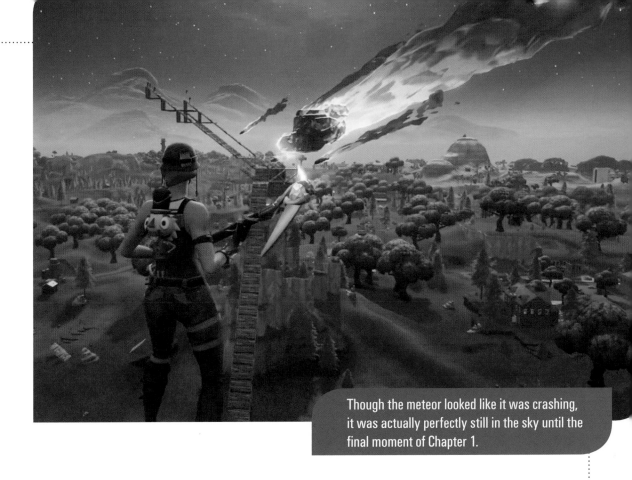

Though the meteor looked like it was crashing, it was actually perfectly still in the sky until the final moment of Chapter 1.

At the same time, a rocket was being constructed at an area of the island called Dusty Depot. Players could also observe a giant meteor frozen in place high in the sky above the island. Everyone knew that these events had to be leading to something, but no one was sure what it would be. Fans debated online and studied the game for clues.

Finally, the big moment arrived. Players who were in the game were treated to an event unlike anything ever seen in *Fortnite* before. Sirens began ringing out across the island, and soon the ground began to rumble. The rocket launched from Dusty Depot and shot up into the darkened sky. High above the ground, it exploded, seemingly causing a rift to form. Soon, other rifts began appearing all across the sky. Rockets began flying out of the rifts and zooming across the island. Eventually, these rockets all gathered around the fro-

Knocked up into the sky, players could see clearly as the island was sucked into a black hole.

As a competitive multiplayer game, *Fortnite* is not generally very heavy on storytelling. Players spend almost all of their time in battles instead of watching story scenes or reading dialogue. But that doesn't mean there's no story in the game. Plenty of things happen in the world of *Fortnite*, and events often carry across multiple seasons. They just tend to happen in the background.

The game never clearly explains what is happening in the storyline. Instead, the **developers** leave hints for players to find, analyze, and debate. Players who choose to ignore the story can simply enjoy the game's exciting battles. But those who are interested can search the island for clues about what is happening. For example, in the first season of Chapter 2, there is a mysterious house containing a variety of souvenirs from the Chapter 1 island. What could this mean? Only time will tell.

zen meteor and then exploded in front of it, forming a single huge rift. The meteor sprung to life and moved into the giant rift. At this point, it seemed to disappear.

Then, yet another rift appeared high in the sky. A red laser shot down from the rift and created a shockwave as it hit the surface of the island. This knocked all the players into the air, where they had a clear view of the events that were unfolding. The meteor emerged from the giant rift and began falling straight toward the ground. When it landed, an enormous explosion sent beams of energy zooming out from the center of the island. All of a sudden, everything around it started being sucked toward the point where the meteor had crashed. Bits and pieces of the island, characters, and even the Battle Bus itself all went hurtling toward one central point. Finally, there was nothing left on the screen. *Fortnite* had disappeared into a black hole.

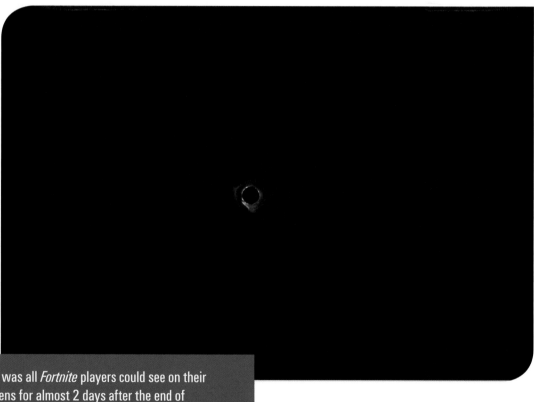

This was all *Fortnite* players could see on their screens for almost 2 days after the end of Chapter 1.

After the black hole appeared, there was no way to play *Fortnite*. When players launched the game, all they saw was a small black hole surrounded by swirling blue light at the center of the screen. Soft, mysterious music played in the background. But that didn't stop millions of people from logging in to watch the black hole, hoping to see something happen.

Epic Games, the developers behind *Fortnite*, announced that this was "the end." But what could that mean? There was no way a game as successful as *Fortnite* was ending forever. How long would it be until people were able to play again? And what would the game even be like once it returned? Fans and **streamers** were left with little to do but compare theories and search for clues about what could be happening. The developers at Epic kept quiet, refusing to explain what was going on.

The event made huge waves around the world, drawing even more attention than usual to *Fortnite*. Major newspapers and video game websites all reported on the "end" of *Fortnite*. But as most fans predicted, it wasn't really the end at all. Instead, it was the start of something new.

Chapter 2

A Fresh Start

Finally, after about 36 hours, the black hole event ended. An update was released for *Fortnite*, and the game came back online. As players logged in to the newly updated game for the first time, they were greeted with an introductory video. It starts with the black hole, which explodes outward into a new universe. Then, a team of *Fortnite* characters appears.

The introductory video of Chapter 2 gave players a hint of how different the new island would be.

You can find weapons of all rarity levels while fishing.

The characters go fishing, drive speedboats, and explore an island full of new locations.

Finally, at the end of the video, a character jumps from the Battle Bus toward the new island. But this isn't just any character. It is the character of the player who was watching the video. And after a couple seconds, it becomes clear that this isn't a video anymore. It has seamlessly transitioned into a real Battle Royale match! This fun surprise caught many players off guard. It was an exciting way to launch players into the world of *Fortnite* Chapter 2.

Right away, players could see that a lot had changed since the last time they played. To begin with, the information and graphics displayed onscreen looked different than before. For example, the health and shield meters were now positioned off to the left side of the screen, instead of at the center. There was also a new bar running along the entire bottom of the screen.

These changes offered a hint at some of the many ways the game's systems were adjusted for the new

Even the main lobby screen got a fresh new look for Chapter 2.

Under the new XP system, almost everything you do in a match will count toward leveling up your Battle Pass.

chapter. The new bar along the bottom of the screen tracks XP, a system of points that allows players to level up their Battle Pass. The Battle Pass has been a part of *Fortnite* for a long time, but the XP-based leveling system is much simpler now. In Chapter 1, there were two things players could earn: Battle Stars and XP. Battle Stars usually came from completing challenges. For example, one challenge might require players to defeat a certain number of enemies at a specific location on the island. Another might require them to open a certain number of treasure chests.

Time to Grind

One of the biggest complaints from players in earlier *Fortnite* seasons was that they needed to spend a lot of time grinding, or completing repetitive tasks over and over again, to reach high levels of the Battle Pass. When the developers at Epic Games introduced changes to the leveling system in Chapter 2, they promised "more fun, less grind." However, many players found the opposite. They were gaining levels more slowly with the new system. Players voiced their concern online, and Epic responded by increasing the amount of experience players could earn from different activities. Any time developers make big changes to an online game like *Fortnite*, they can accidentally create new problems. Sorting everything out can sometimes be a matter of trial and error.

XP was awarded to players when they defeated enemies, won a Victory Royale, or completed other basic goals in a match. After gaining enough XP, the player's "season level" would go up. The season level was different from the Battle Pass level. Each season level would reward players with a few Battle Stars. After gaining 10 stars through challenges or season levels, the Battle Pass level would go up by 1. If this sounds confusing or complicated, that's because it was!

The leveling system in *Fortnite* Chapter 2 is much simpler. Whether you complete a challenge or achieve some other goal in the game, you'll simply receive XP. There are no more Battle Stars. Gaining XP will cause the bar at the bottom of the screen to fill up. Once it is full, your Battle Pass level will go up by one. This means XP is the only thing you need to keep track of. You can earn it by completing the same kinds of challenges that have always been in *Fortnite*. You can also earn small amounts of XP from simple things such as opening treasure chests or visiting new areas of the map.

Chapter 2 also adds another way to gain XP quickly. Each day, you can work to fill up a Medal Punchcard. Medals are awarded for excelling at a certain aspect of the game. For example, you can earn a Scavenger Medal by opening three treasure chests in one match. Earning a medal gives you bonus XP. You can also upgrade your medals by continuing to do the thing that earned you the medal in the first place. So if you want to upgrade your Scavenger Medal, keep opening chests. Upgraded medals will give you huge amounts of XP!

There are all kinds of medals to earn. Some involve defeating enemies or staying alive in matches. Others involve using certain weapons or scavenging for supplies. Your Medal Punchcard has room for up to eight medals per day. It resets each day, so you have to start all over again each time. Gaining medals is one of the fastest ways to earn XP and level up your Battle Pass, so it is worth the effort.

The faster, simpler leveling system is not the only change to the way *Fortnite* works in Chapter 2. One small but very convenient improvement comes at the end of each match. Whether you win a Victory Royale or get defeated early on, you no longer have to go back to the lobby screen before joining a new game.

Earning medals will help you gain experience very quickly.

This means you can get back into the action very quickly after each match.

You might also notice that your first few matches in Chapter 2 seem either easier or harder than normal. You aren't imagining things. Epic Games has made some adjustments to the way *Fortnite* picks which players get grouped in a match together. It now tries to match up players with similar levels of skill and experience. In other words, new players are less likely to run into seasoned pros, and players who perform well are more likely to get grouped with people with similar skills.

Epic also added bots to *Fortnite*. Bots are computer-controlled players. They are used to fill up matches when a few players are needed to get things started. This helps make sure there are always new matches started, so players don't have to wait. Bots are not usually very good players. They have poor aim and they are not good at building. If you have any experience with the game, you will probably be able to defeat them easily. However, there is no easy way to tell a bot apart from a real player until you start battling. Bots have realistic usernames and wear all kinds of skins. So don't let your guard down!

Chapter 3

Finding Your Way

Perhaps the biggest change of all in *Fortnite* Chapter 2 is the new island. The original *Fortnite* island went through a lot of changes from season to season, but it always kept the same basic shape and layout. In Chapter 2, that island was replaced with an entirely new one. That means everyone from new players to *Fortnite* experts had a lot of exploring to do once Chapter 2 kicked off.

A giant waterfall is one of the most impressive features of the new island.

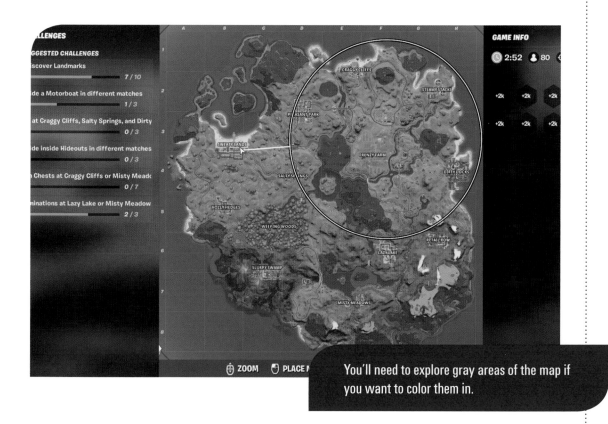

You'll need to explore gray areas of the map if you want to color them in.

Upon landing on the new island, many players likely opened their map screens to see where they should go. But that would only reveal another surprise of the new chapter. The map screen now starts off completely gray. Instead of labels naming the different areas of the map, there are just question marks. Players have to travel to each area of the map to color it in and see its name. Once they visit a new part of the map, it will stay colored in for all future matches. This means players have to explore the entire island over the course of a few matches if they want to have a complete map.

Chapter 2 also added new map features called landmarks. Landmarks are smaller locations in between the main named areas of the island. Discovering a new one fills in a small part of the map and rewards players with XP, so it is worth seeking them out.

Scattered across the island are several new features players can use to gain an advantage over their opponents. First, there are now upgrade benches hidden away inside many buildings. At these benches,

Finding a new landmark will help fill in your map and give you a nice XP boost.

Not all of the changes in Chapter 2 are additions to the game. In fact, the update removed quite a few familiar things from the world of *Fortnite*. Most of the game's vehicles are gone. There are no more giant robots to pilot. Even some of the game's common weapons, such as the suppressed pistol and the heavy assault rifle, were put back in the vault.

Why would *Fortnite*'s developers choose to remove all these things from the game? Many players felt like the game had become full of side activities that distracted from the basic battling and building that made *Fortnite* unique. There were also concerns that all the additions had **unbalanced** the game. By simplifying and going back to the basics of *Fortnite*, the developers were able to focus on the things that made the game fun in the first place.

players can trade building materials to upgrade one of their weapons to the next highest level of rarity. For example, you could turn a green uncommon weapon into a blue rare weapon.

There are also new containers to loot. Large ammo boxes contain more ammo than the standard boxes players are already familiar with. Blue treasure chests are another Chapter 2 addition. These chests are rarer than the standard ones, and they always hold either a purple epic or orange legendary weapon.

There is also a completely new type of weapon. The Bandage Bazooka is unlike any other *Fortnite* weapon. Instead of damaging enemies, its shots can be used to heal teammates or your own character. Unlike other weapons, it takes up two inventory slots. This means you will be very limited in what else you can carry if you decide to pick it up.

Another new item is the fishing rod. You are very likely to come across a fishing rod soon after you start playing Chapter 2, as it is a very common tool. Use it to cast a line into one of the island's many waterways. You can catch a variety of fish that restore health and shields. If you're lucky, you can also reel in some powerful weapons.

Speaking of water, Chapter 2 added the ability to swim. And if you don't feel like swimming, you can always look for a boat. Boats are a really fast way to get around on the new island. Almost all the major areas on the map are connected by a series of rivers, lakes, and streams. Boats are also equipped with weapons, so you can fight back if someone attacks you on the water.

Do you like to play Duos or Squads? Chapter 2 added a new feature that will change your team strategies. Now, when a player gets knocked down, you can

Boats are the fastest way to travel across the new island.

pick them up and carry them. This means you can pick up teammates and take them to a safe location before healing them. It also means you can pick up enemies after they get knocked down! Take a knocked down enemy to a location that will draw their teammates into a trap. Or simply throw your captured enemy off a cliff to knock them out of the round for good. There are all kinds of ways to be creative with this new feature, so feel free to experiment.

Chapter 4

What's Next?

t will surely take a while for players to uncover all of the hidden details of *Fortnite* Chapter 2. But one thing is for sure: It won't be long before Epic starts making even more changes to the game. The new island will grow and change just like the old one did.

Chapter 2 added an achievement list to *Fortnite*. Achievements are fun awards that show up on your career profile when you complete certain tasks in the game.

New Looks for a New Chapter

Of course, it wouldn't be a *Fortnite* update without new skins, **emotes**, and other fun ways to customize your character. Chapter 2 introduced a whole bunch of colorful new character skins to unlock through the Battle Pass and purchase in the in-game store.

There are also special new emotes that multiple players can join together to perform. For example, if you unlock the High Five emote, you can approach another player in-game and activate it. Both characters will then high five each other. More complex emotes like this one will likely be added to the game in the future.

And now that they've replaced the island completely, they could do it again in the future. You never know what's going to happen next in *Fortnite*. That's a big part of what makes it so fun!

But even with all the big changes to Battle Royale mode in Chapter 2, *Fortnite*'s other two modes have mostly stayed the same so far. Creative mode and Save the World are continuing to get minor updates, but they still work pretty much exactly the same as they did in Chapter 1. It makes sense that Epic would update Battle Royale first. After all, it is by far the most popular mode. But it seems like a safe bet that big changes will eventually come to the other modes as well.

Fortnite's seasons will continue to change every 2 to 3 months. Smaller changes will come in between the big seasonal updates, too, as Epic listens to player feedback and makes adjustments. What would you like to see next in *Fortnite*? Do you have ideas for new features to add to the game? Or maybe you'd like just a slight change to the way something works in the current game. Share your opinions online. Discuss your ideas with friends. You never know what will

Have an idea for another new weapon like the Bandage Bazooka? Let other *Fortnite* fans know!

It's time to board the Battle Bus and start fighting your way through Chapter 2!

happen. The developers at Epic Games pay attention to the things players are saying, and your idea could become popular with other *Fortnite* fans. With any luck, you could see some incredible changes in *Fortnite* Chapter 3, 4, or beyond.

Of course, the most important thing is to have fun while you play. Round up your friends, get online, and start exploring the island!

Glossary

developers (dih-VEL-uh-purz) people who make video games or other computer programs

emotes (EE-mohts) animations a character can perform in an online video game to communicate with other players

skins (SKINZ) different appearances your character can take on in *Fortnite*

streamers (STREEM-urz) people who broadcast live video feeds of themselves playing video games for others to watch online

unbalanced (uhn-BAL-uhnsd) an unbalanced game has features that give some players an unfair advantage

Find Out More

BOOKS

Cunningham, Kevin. *Video Game Designer*. Ann Arbor, MI: Cherry Lake Publishing, 2016.

Powell, Marie. *Asking Questions About Video Games*. Ann Arbor, MI: Cherry Lake Publishing, 2016.

WEBSITES

Epic Games—Fortnite
www.epicgames.com/fortnite/en-US/home
Check out the official *Fortnite* website.

Fortnite Wiki
https://fortnite.gamepedia.com/Fortnite_Wiki
This fan-made website offers up-to-date information on the latest additions to *Fortnite*.

Index

About the Author

Josh Gregory is the author of more than 150 books for kids. He has written about everything from animals to technology to history. A graduate of the University of Missouri–Columbia, he currently lives in Chicago, Illinois.